DOLPHINS SET II

Risso's Dolphins

Kristin Petrie
ABDO Publishing Company

visit us at
www.abdopub.com

Published by ABDO Publishing Company, 4940 Viking Drive, Edina, Minnesota 55435.
Copyright © 2006 by Abdo Consulting Group, Inc. International copyrights reserved in all countries. No part of this book may be reproduced in any form without written permission from the publisher. The Checkerboard Library™ is a trademark and logo of ABDO Publishing Company.

Printed in the United States.

Cover Photo: © Michael S. Nolan / SeaPics.com
Interior Photos: © Danny Frank / SeaPics.com p. 8; © Joao Quaresma / SeaPics.com pp. 12, 19; © Kike Calvo / V&W / SeaPics.com p. 17; © Michael S. Nolan / SeaPics.com p. 13; © Phillip Colla / SeaPics.com pp. 10, 21; © Robert L. Pitman / SeaPics.com p. 5; © Tom Campbell / SeaPics.com p. 15; Uko Gorter p. 7

Series Coordinator: Megan M. Gunderson
Editors: Megan M. Gunderson, Megan Murphy
Art Direction, Diagram, & Map: Neil Klinepier

Library of Congress Cataloging-in-Publication Data

Petrie, Kristin, 1970-
   Risso's dolphins / Kristin Petrie.
      p. cm. -- (Dolphins. Set II)
   ISBN 1-59679-303-1 (hardcover)
   1. Risso's dolphin--Juvenile literature. I. Title.

QL737.C432P4665 2005
599.53--dc22
                                                          2005046214

CONTENTS

Risso's Dolphins

All dolphins are mammals. Like humans, dolphins are born with hair, they nurse their young with milk, and they breathe air. Though it looks a bit like a whale or a porpoise, the *Grampus griseus* is a kind of dolphin. It is more commonly known as the Risso's dolphin.

Risso's dolphins are part of the **family** Delphinidae. This is the largest family of **cetaceans**. It includes the bottlenose dolphin and the killer whale. The Delphinidae family is broken into smaller groups, too. So, Risso's dolphins are also part of the subfamily Delphininae.

The name *Grampus griseus* comes from Latin and possibly other languages. *Grampus* means "large fish." Risso's dolphins get the second part of their name from their **unique** coloring. *Griseus* means "grizzled, mottled with gray."

Risso's dolphins sometimes share their habitat with bottlenose dolphins.

SIZE, SHAPE, AND COLOR

Adult Risso's dolphins are usually about 10 feet (3 m) long. But, they may grow to 12 feet (4 m) in length. Males are usually longer than females. Risso's dolphins weigh about 650 pounds (300 kg) or more. Some weigh up to 1,100 pounds (500 kg).

Many dolphins can be identified by their long snout. However, Risso's dolphins don't have this feature. Instead, they have a crease that runs down their broad **melon** from the forehead to the mouth. The mouth slants up. So, Risso's dolphins are always smiling!

The Risso's dolphin has a sleek, barrel-shaped body. Its round body narrows to a strong, wide tail fin. The **flukes** have a distinctive center notch. The **dorsal** fin is tall and curved with a wide base and a pointy tip. The chest flippers are long and skinny and point straight back.

Risso's dolphins vary in color from dark gray to brown. They may become all white as they age. This is from hundreds of scars that cover their bodies. These scars are from **parasites** and from the teeth of other dolphins. They also have a large, anchor-shaped white mark on their bellies.

MELON

EYE

FLIPPER

DORSAL FIN

FLUKE

WHERE THEY LIVE

Changes in their habitats have caused some Risso's dolphins to find new homes.

Risso's dolphins are found all over the globe. Some like warm, tropical water. Others prefer more **temperate** water. They are found in the Atlantic, Pacific, and Indian oceans. They are also found in the Mediterranean Sea and the Red Sea.

Risso's dolphins usually stay away from shore. Their favorite hangouts are along **continental shelves**. Occasionally, some Risso's dolphins will venture closer to shore. This is most likely around islands. The shelf is smaller there, so they are already nearer the shore.

Scientists do not know for sure if Risso's dolphins **migrate**. If they do, they probably do not travel far. These dolphins have been known to travel with the changing seasons. Or, they may just be following their food supply.

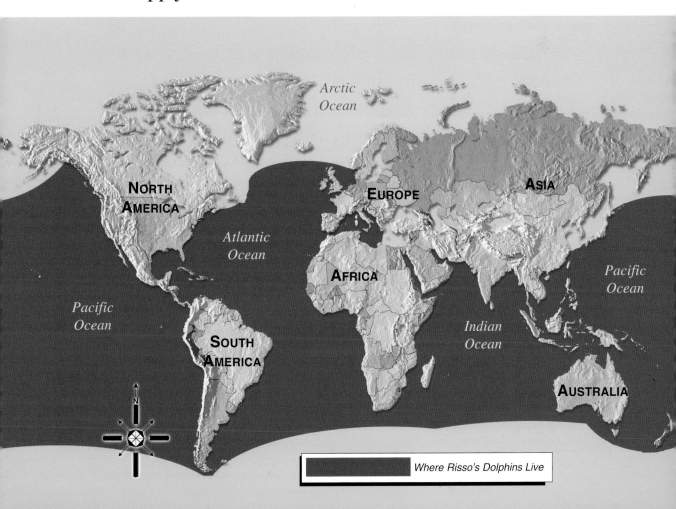

Where Risso's Dolphins Live

SENSES

An ocean is a big home. So, Risso's dolphins use all their senses to keep from getting lost in their **habitat**. Like most **cetaceans**, they use echolocation to find their way.

Echolocation is like a high-tech navigation system. Dolphins make sounds that shoot through the water. When these sounds reach an object, they bounce off, or echo. The echoed noise returns to the mammal as information.

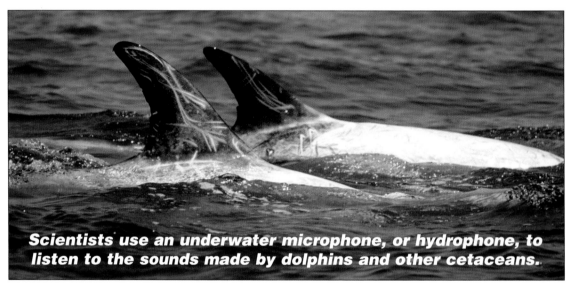

Scientists use an underwater microphone, or hydrophone, to listen to the sounds made by dolphins and other cetaceans.

Dolphins use echolocation to find prey and avoid **predators**. The noises dolphins make for echolocation are **unique**. So, they can sometimes be used to identify a particular dolphin species. Other noises are used for communication with their friends!

Sound wave sent out by dolphin

Echo wave received by dolphin

DEFENSE

Unfortunately, echolocation can't help Risso's dolphins avoid every danger. Fishing nets are one of their main threats. Water pollution also threatens their watery home. And in some areas, this species is hunted by humans. They have little defense against these threats.

A dolphin's melon may be used to help direct the sounds used in echolocation.

Luckily, Risso's dolphins are thriving in most areas. Scientists used to think these dolphins were rare. This may be partly because they stay far from shore. But now, Risso's dolphins are believed to be quite common.

The total worldwide population of Risso's dolphins is unknown. There are more than 250,000 in the Pacific Ocean. Up to 30,000 Risso's dolphins may live off the coast of California alone. And, scientists think there are almost as many off the East Coast of the United States.

Risso's dolphins use their teeth for playing and fighting. This adds to the scarring on their skin.

Food

A Risso's dolphin's favorite food is squid! Huge squid, up to 12 feet (4 m) long, have fallen prey to the Risso's dolphin. This species will also settle for fish, **crustaceans**, and octopuses when needed.

Catching squid is tricky work. Risso's dolphins work together for this job. They cooperate by swimming side by side in a long line. This helps them catch more prey.

Risso's dolphins often hunt in deep water. And they eat mostly at night. This is when some of their prey swims up near the surface.

Risso's dolphins have seven pairs of teeth or fewer in their lower jaw. Typically, there are no teeth in the upper jaw. Like other similar **cetaceans**, Risso's dolphins probably use their teeth to snatch food but not to chew it.

Risso's dolphins and their close relatives swallow their food whole!

BABIES

Not much is known about the mating of Risso's dolphins. They start mating when they are eight to nine feet (2 to 3 m) in length. Scientists think the dolphins are around 13 years of age at this time.

Female Risso's dolphins are **pregnant** for 13 to 14 months. They can give birth at any time of the year. Like other mammals of this size, Risso's dolphins usually give birth to one baby dolphin at a time.

Baby dolphins are called calves. Risso's dolphin calves are usually four to five feet (1 to 1.5 m) long at birth. Calves stay near their mothers after they are born.

As they grow, the calves are nursed with milk. Later, they will hunt for squid like other adult Risso's dolphins. In the wild, Risso's dolphins can live for 20 years or more.

From a distance, some young Risso's dolphins can be mistaken for killer whales or bottlenose dolphins.

BEHAVIORS

Some dolphins are loners. However, Risso's dolphins may travel in crowds of 1,000 or more! Occasionally, they swim in groups of 100 to 200. But most often, these dolphins are found in **pods** of 3 to 50. Risso's dolphins are also known to mingle with other dolphin species.

Risso's dolphins swim slowly near the surface of the water. But occasionally, they will have bursts of energy. Risso's dolphins enjoy **breaching**, **spyhopping**, and slapping the surface of the water with their **flukes**. And sometimes, they splash and strike each other.

One Risso's dolphin was very famous. His name was Pelorus Jack. This smart dolphin escorted ships through Cook Strait in New Zealand for 24 years. He became so famous that a law was passed to protect him.

Risso's dolphins are most often found in water with a surface temperature of 50 to 82 degrees Fahrenheit (10 to 28˚C).

Risso's Dolphin Facts

Scientific Name: *Grampus griseus*

Common Names: Grampus, Grey Grampus, White-Head Grampus, Gray Dolphin

Average Size: Around 10 feet (3 m) long and 650 pounds (300 kg). Males are typically larger than females.

Where They're Found: Temperate and tropical areas of the Pacific, Atlantic, and Indian oceans, and the Mediterranean and Red seas

At all ages, Risso's dolphins have dark fins and flukes, as well as a dark patch around each eye.

GLOSSARY

breach - to jump or leap up out of the water.

cetacean (sih-TAY-shuhn) - any of various types of mammal, such as the dolphin, that live in water like fish.

continental shelf - a shallow, underwater plain that borders a continent and ends with a steep slope to the ocean floor.

crustacean (kruhs-TAY-shuhn) - any of a group of animals with hard shells that live mostly in water. Crabs, lobsters, and shrimps are all crustaceans.

dorsal - located near or on the back, especially of an animal.

family - a group that scientists use to classify similar plants or animals. It ranks above a genus and below an order.

fluke - either of the fins that make up the tail of a cetacean, such as a whale or dolphin.

habitat - a place where a living thing is naturally found.

melon - the rounded forehead of some cetaceans, which may aid in echolocation.

migrate - to move from one place to another, often to find food.

parasite - an organism that lives off of another organism of a different species.

pod - a group of animals, typically whales or dolphins.

predator - an animal that kills and eats other animals.

pregnant - having one or more babies growing within the body.

spyhop - to raise the head above water to look around.

temperate - having neither very hot nor very cold weather.

unique - being the only one of its kind.

WEB SITES

To learn more about Risso's dolphins, visit ABDO Publishing Company on the World Wide Web at **www.abdopub.com**. Web sites about these dolphins are featured on our Book Links page. These links are routinely monitored and updated to provide the most current information available.

INDEX

A

Atlantic Ocean 8, 13

B

bottlenose dolphin 4

C

calves 4, 16
color 4, 7

D

defense 11, 12
Delphinidae 4
Delphininae 4
dorsal fin 6

E

echolocation 10, 11, 12

F

flippers 6
flukes 6, 18
food 4, 9, 11, 14, 16

H

habitat 8, 10
head 6
hunting 11, 14, 16

I

Indian Ocean 8

K

killer whale 4

L

life span 16

M

mammals 4, 10, 16
mating 16
Mediterranean Sea 8
melon 6
migration 9
mouth 6

N

New Zealand 18

P

Pacific Ocean 8, 13
parasites 7
Pelorus Jack 18
pods 18
population 12, 13
predators 11

R

Red Sea 8

S

scars 7
senses 10, 11
size 6, 16
snout 6
sounds 10, 11
speed 18

T

teeth 7, 14
threats 12

U

United States 13

24